ON THE BLACK HAND SIDE

GERALD L. COLEMAN

Iconiclast Press
Atlanta, Georgia

ISBN 978-1-0878-6859-2

Geraldcoleman.com

Cover Image by Erica Willey
Cover Design by Erica Willey and Gerald L. Coleman

for affrilachia ...

Contents

introduction

I am human. My life matters. This is the message I am attempting to communicate in this collection. I don't believe that art can somehow transform any human being. Racists aren't sitting around waiting on the right poem, song, or painting to change them. But I do believe that people of good will, open to the possibility of evolving, willing to listen and learn, to be confronted with hard truths about themselves, can be transformed by art.

We aren't living in a new age of awakening. We are still fighting the same battles. It's a trick of post modernity and what Jean-François Lyotard would call a reflection of High Modernism in which the justification of scientific work is not to create an adequate model of what *is* - ontologically speaking, but rather to simply generate more - to produce fresh *énoncés*. It allows people to say, *look how far we've come*, as an elaborate stalling mechanism, while they continue to benefit from the same systems and structures that buoyed their grandfathers, and their grandfathers. My hope is to clarify. To pull back the veil. To simplify the question for you. I am either human or I am not. And if I am, then what?

The other thing to know about my work is that I believe in accessible art. I'm not interested, on the whole, in complex forms and structures that become shibboleths for literati showing off for one another - what Lyotard calls the *taking of tricks:*

> *[T]he linguistic dimensions of what used to be called French structuralism and the seemingly more static possibilities of a dominant semiotics have in recent years been corrected and augmented by a return to pragmatics, to the analysis of language situations and games, and of language itself as an unstable exchange between its speakers, whose utterances are now seen less and less as a process of transmission of information or messages, or in terms of some network of signs or signifying systems, than as (to use one of Lyotard's favorite figures) the "taking of tricks," the trumping of a communicational adversary, an essentially conflictual relationship between tricksters - and not as a well-regulated and noisefree "passing of tokens from hand to hand" (Mallarmé on denotative speech).*
>
> ~ *Fredric Jameson*

I prefer egalitarian art - art that can be accessed and enjoyed by everyone. In other words, my attempt is to pass noisefree tokens from my hand to yours.

This collection began as most due, with individual poems. I write poetry to process what's going on in the world in general, and in my life in particular. Usually, when the number reaches a certain inevitable mass, I begin thinking about publishing them as a collection - if they have some internal cohering. As I looked at the poetry that made its way into this collection, I realized that I was trying to get a something singular, something particular - that I am a human being. That black people are human beings. We aren't stereotypes, subhuman, or outside of the exigencies that preoccupy you. We love our children as much as you love yours. We want a safe place to live as much as you do. We want to eat good food, drink good drink, vacation in that beautiful place, get a good interest rate on our home loan. We want all the things you want. But we live in country that makes it its business to help you get those things and to stand in the way of us getting them too. America has always been a zero-sum enterprise, built for the elevation of one group at the expense of others. But maybe if you recognize our common humanity, you'll see the world more clearly. And maybe, just maybe, you'll help change the world.

I hope my poetry is a step along the way.

Gerald L. Coleman
March 2022
Atlanta, Georgia

ON THE BLACK HAND SIDE

on the black hand side

meet me
on
the black hand
side
where lives evaporate
like
dust in a sandstorm
of hate and
apathy
is a crown
worn
by the fair

love me
on
the black hand side
where i skip
two ropes
at a time
because one
would waste my time
listen
to my sing
song
as I smear joy
on myself
because no one else
will

grease in my
hair
lotion
on my skin
and my mama
checking to see
if i'm
in the house
because the street lights
are on
or because
i'm grown
and black
and the world
thinks its white

mourn me
on
the black hand side
because
my life
didn't matter
enough
to be thought of
as human

absence makes the heart

i wish
that i
could tell
11 year old
me
that you'll be
better
without him

i wish i could
hug him
and whisper
in his tiny
ear
you'll be a better man
because
he won't be around
to drown you
in his toxic
view
of manhood

the pain
seems unbearable
now
because you want
your father around
but if you

can hang on
for just
a little while
it will become
clear
that it was
a gift
freeing you
from him
and his father
and his before him
and all the carnage
they carried
with them

but i can't
go back
and save him
from what
is coming
he will have to
get by
on a mama's love
and a boy's
tears
the anger
will be
unavoidable

but
i gaze back
in time

and console myself
by knowing
one day
he will be free

first kiss

i kissed
tonya
behind the corner
store
when i was
eleven

we were riding
our bikes
together
after school
and stopped
to stare
in each other's eyes
without a word
and
we reached
for the unknown
across our
handle bars

it was
as sweet
as a jolly rancher
cherry
or watermelon
and
the world disappeared

into
racing heartbeats
and
newly born
delight

it was as pure
as
saturday morning cartoons
not the kind
of hunger
or want
in grown tongues
naked abandon
the ecstasy
of trying to climb
inside
another

just
the simple
tartness
of young
infatuation
the birth
of something
dreamed about
in confusion
and anticipation

i kissed
tonya

behind the corner
store
in secret
and rode
my bike
on the fuel
of the discovery
of her
lips
for hours

love, peace, & hair grease

was the world
a better place
than in
summer

school was out
sleeping was in
with no supervison
latchkey kids
abandoned to our own
imaginations
until 3:30 pm

building go carts
tree forts
bows and arrows
for the empty fields
behind our houses
flimsy
wood ramps
on shaky cinder blocks
for bmx bikes
without helmets
or knee pads
kickflips on skateboards
in vacant parking lots

on bumblegum and candy bars
dungeons & dragons
on friday nights
the comic book store
on saturday
but first

hair grease

i kept my hair
long
so my summer
always began
with my mama's
hands
in my head

have you ever
had your hair
parted
by someone who
loves you
running their finger
along your
scalp
with warm
hair grease
that smelled like
joy
and freedom
with
let's get serious

playing in the
background?

my plaits
rows
of simple
three stranded braids
were 5,000 years
in the making
from a time
when
they spoke of age, tribe
wealth
and marital status
down the nile valley
they came
across the sahel
from the fula
as far south as
namibia
and beyond
until
slavers came

once
beautiful
intricate
narratives woven
in expressed dna
became shaved heads
as white men
tried to mar our beauty

to un-tan-gle us
from who we were
the complex became
simple
plaits
of convenience
greased in kerosene
because time
was no longer
ours
but belonged
to someone else
and we learned
to make do

those
simple twists of fate
endured
came to rest
on my head
every summer
by way
of
my mother's nimble fingers
because time
was not her's
or mine
but the love
i felt
sitting between her legs
at the beginning of summer
while she tugged

my mane
into ancient weaves
was
and so was the history
radiant
upon my head

was the world
ever
a better place
than
in summer?

that poor woman

(for my mom)

the nurses
knew
my name

i'd made
so many trips
to
the emergency room
that summer
they knew
it was me

what did he do now?

before
i blew myself up
i was
at a ballpark
in
the bottoms
and this time
all i'd wanted
was
ice cream

we were on
the playground

next to
the ballpark
when
the dulcet tones
of
the ice cream truck
drifted
to our ears
on
a warm
summer breeze

so we ran
we ran
to find our
moms
to plead
our case
for money
because
there are only
two
immutable forces
in the universe
when
you're twelve
saturday morning
cartoons
and
the ice cream man

so we ran

enjambment echoes the breathless, pure nature of childhood joy

16

a rabid
gallery
of adolescences
in sneakers and
faded tshirts
riven
by the undeniable
desire
for a bomb pop
or an orange
pushup

everyone else
ran around
the chain
meant ostensibly
to keep cars
from driving through
but i
decided to jump
to fly
like shazam
or leap
like daredevil
and
i miscalculated

the poor
woman
entrusted
with my parentage
was minding

her own business
watching the game
in the stands
when
the loud speaker
announced
for the whole stadium
to hear
will the mother
of gerald coleman
please report
to the playground

she found me
laid out
in front
of a car
prostrate
unconscious
unmoving
with a coat
rolled up
under my head
a knot
the size
of a tangerine
on my forehead
thinking
he's done it
this time
he's killed
himself

the rock fights
bottle cap zip
guns
jumping off
rooves
an exploding gas tank
rickety
handmade go karts
bike jumps
off tenuous
wooden ramps
had all failed
to kill me
but this time
she knew
i'd succeeded
until
i woke up
dazed and confused
with a crowd
of faces
looking down
at me

once again
it was nurses
who knew
my name
shaking their heads
and hugging
my mom

because
that poor woman
had
a child
who'd be
the death of her
if america
didn't
kill me
first

difference engine

what happens
when
your handmade
wooden
go kart's wheel
comes off
halfway
down the hill?

you learn

you learn
about axles
how bolts
and hex nuts
are better
than
a handful of nails
for keeping
your scavenged
big wheel and
radio flyer wheels on

this is
a true story
about learning
halfway
down the hill

exposition trickles into interiors, demonstrates that the institutional cannot be unlinked from the individual

by trent
and niagara drive

in the 1820s
charles babbage
designed
the difference engine
to make
a series of calculations
with multiple variables
it was
a machine
meant
to solve
a singular
complex problem
you see
you learn
when exposed
to multiple variables
of the same
singular
horror
you learn
to keep
your guard up
to distrust
teachers
nurses
clerks
cops
and friends

because
they dont see you
as
human

you learn
to check your food
to get
a third opinion
to have
a family member
guard your bed
and your chart
at the hospital
how to
report
a racist professor
who thinks
you couldn't have
written this paper
to hold
your hands
out the window
because
you don't
want to die
over
a traffic stop

you learn
that
being black

a conceit
↳ engine is a conceit
for the multivariable
experience of blackness

23

is a singular
problem
with
multiple variables
in need
of
a complex
difference engine
to calculate
whether
you will
make it home
safe

INTERLUDE one

wonder twin powers activate

I can't remember the first comic I read. That memory is wrapped up in discovering science fiction and fantasy at the Scholastic book fair. And that memory is wrapped up in my mother reading The Jungle Book, by Rudyard Kipling, to my brother and I to get us to fall asleep, Saturday morning cartoons, and my uncle giving me Conan the Barbarian comics and novels. I was the kid yelling, "*Wonder Twin powers activate,*" "*Shazam,*" and "*O zephyr winds which blow on high / Lift me now so I can fly*" Saturday afternoon in the parking lot of our apartment complex on 4th street. I was also the kid who made Space Ghost gauntlets out of construction paper so I could press those three buttons and fire off imaginary blasts. There was also the animated Rikki-Tikki-Tavi adaptation by Chuck Jones in 1975. That was my favorite animated special. I never missed it anytime it was on tv. It all combined to deeply enthrall and enmesh me, irrevocably, into comic books.

And, eventually, science fiction and fantasy. Somewhere in there were reruns of the original Star Trek tv show. It all led to me spending my entire allowance in a comic book store.

I wish I could remember the name. By the time I was in college, I was buying comics from the Comic Connection on Limestone, across from the University of Kentucky Hospital. But early on, there was a store down by the old bus station, near third street where my love of comics was ignited. What I can remember is the smell. It was a hole in the wall, one of a dozen musty storefronts lined up like books on a forgotten shelf in the attic, that smelled of dust and fresh ink. I can still smell it all these years later. I can also remember the unfettered awe of seeing all those boxes and boxes of comics. They were identical to the singular, long, white box I still have that contains the last vestiges of my collection. In that box are issues of Alpha Flight, X-men, the Teenage Mutant Ninja Turtles, Prince Namor, and an assortment of all manner of other titles.

If I'd been able, I would've spent hundreds, even thousands of dollars in that small shop. It was like a Scholastic Book Fair for comics, but open every day of the week, and it was just as magical to a young me. I could browse for hours if

I'd had the time, but my mom was waiting in the car for me. She had grocery shopping to do and other errands to run, but she made time for me to stop and get my comics. We'd also be stopping at the dairy queen on broadway for a footlong or a vanilla cone dipped in chocolate, and the whistle stop pop shop for bottle soda — grape and orange for me. That was my saturday afternoon.

I couldn't believe there were so many comics. The Avengers, Thor, Daredevil, Power Man and Iron Fist, the X-men, Spider-man, and on and on. There was a long table with the newest issues laid out, and racks with even more recent editions. I'd spend my entire allowance and leave with my brown paper bag as thick as phone book (that was approximately four inches thick for those of you who have never seen one lol), with each individual comic in its own plastic sleeve. And when I got home, full of footlong and ice cream, I'd go to my room and read for hours — catching up on mutants trying to survive a world full of prejudice, the God of Thunder trying to stave off Ragnarok, Power Man and Iron Fist trying to make rent while fighting mystical forces, and Daredevil cleaning up Hell's Kitchen.

It's likely why I am the way I am. Why I've spent my life unable to walk past and injustice, big or small. Why I took up martial arts, why I hold open doors, and confront assholes who think it's ok to put their hands on women uninvited. It's why I have a deep and abiding sense of who the good guys are and how you deal with bad guys. And it's why courage has been my badge of honor.

Sure, there's a lot to be said about all the other experiences in my life and how they shaped my ideology and self-image. From theology and philosophy at university, to discovering my history and intellectual, cultural, and social inheritance through reading The Autobiography of Malcolm X, the Souls of Black Folk, Things Fall Apart, the writers of the Harlem Renaissance, and all the other pieces of literature those books led me to. But I'd be remiss to not include the impact comic books made on me becoming the man I am today. And how much those Saturday's, in the comic book store, shaped me.

placebo — a treatment with no active properties

we laugh
so that
we do not
die
it is not
a dismissal
or a breach
of etiquette
it is
survival

if we
did not laugh
the world
would drown
in our tears
or burn
in the fire
of our
rage

lamentation

hope
isn't enough
to live on
when the world
only feeds you
rage

the menu
must include
justice

without it
words
turn to ash
on the tongues
of allies
and prophets

and my
prayer
becomes an invitation
to the sun

devour us now

are the kids alright?

some of them
are nazis
not fallen far
from
the nazi tree
watered
with blood
as long as
it's not theirs

are the kids
all right?

some of them
are racists
high
on daddy's priviledge
drunk
on the bigotry in their mama's
milk
in their *jordans*
drinking
fair trade coffee
listening to *anderson .paak*
mad they aren't allowed
to say nigga
because
what they hate

more than anything
is being told
no

are the kids
all right?

their parents aren't
and 1950
was just yesterday

a homily on sacrifice

(because the creative community is infected)

it is no longer
acceptable
to blot out
the sun
forcing others
to live
in a darkness
of your own
making

who told you
zeus
was a hero?
that three-eyed
demons
should be emulated
or did you
decide that shit
on your own?
medusa is the heroine
in this adaptation
crowned queen
for surviving
your bullshit

did someone tell you
iago was the hero?

did you even read
that shit?
or were you just
aroused
by seeing
a black man
lose?

you may no longer
sacrifice us
to the gods
of notoriety
and personal
avarice
now, we
are the ones
with the knives
and the altars

so, yes
you should be scared

on the vagaries of

whiteness

after
spending a thousand
years
telling us
to
gtfoh
why do y'all
get so mad
when we start
something
that's only
for us

make up
your
goddamn
mind

or is whiteness → blackness as communal
also   vs.
co-dependant?   whiteness as co-dependant

INTERLUDE two

the scandal of 1982

It was the end of the summer of 1982. Mom announced that money was tight, so we were only going to get three new outfits for the school year. My brother Tim, sanguine and unbothered by fashion, was nonplussed. He would come to school in a black t-shirt with numbers on the back—an old league basketball shirt— green pants from a church Youth Day outfit, and dirty sneakers. He didn't care.

Looking back, I'm proud of his devil-may-care attitude toward all things even remotely peer pressure. But back then, I would roll my eyes and shake my head when he turned up at the bus stop. It was a problem for me. Now, it wasn't just that I cared about fashion, it was that if someone started talking shit, I'd have to fight. Because as much as he and I fought, we were teenage boys and brothers after all. We had each other's back in a fight. That was just brother code. But I hated to fight in my school clothes.

I was scandalized by my mom's family announcement. What you have to know about me is that I loved clothes. More particularly, I loved looking good. According to my mother, I was three years old when I told her she didn't need to pick out what I was going to wear anymore, I'd do it. Yeah, three. When it came to a new school year, I was the kid who planned out his outfits for the week. Once I'd chosen, after hours of debate, I'd iron everything and lay it out with the shoes at the foot of my bed. New clothes were a part of the excitement of a new year, along with school supplies, the right backpack, and the promise of new classes and meeting new kids.

So, when mom announced there would only be three new outfits, I was inconsolable. But she was a black mom trying to raise two boys on her own and no amount of complaints, displays of dejection, or pouting would sway her. Had I been literarily astute, I might have roamed from room to room in the house, quoting Yeats:

> "But I, being poor, have only my dreams;
> I have spread my dreams under your feet;

Tread softly because you tread on my dreams."

As an adult, I understand. Sometimes money is tight and that's just the way it is. But as a teen, it was like receiving a death sentence in only the way a myopic kid could. I couldn't believe it. The only other family pronouncement that had ever been as devastating was the year she, and my aunts and uncles, announced that all my cousins wouldn't be coming to Lexington for the holidays. We were crushed. For as long as we could remember, the holidays were the time the fourteen of us got together and had the time of our lives. Our parents would drink, play spades or bid whist at the kitchen table, while we ran around like Barnum & Bailey's three ring circus.

We slept in the hallways, on couches, and hung from the proverbial ceiling, there were so many of us in the house. When they all stayed with us, we'd wake up and mom would act like a short order cook, fixing whatever anyone wanted for breakfast. We'd sing, make up dance routines, and get into all kinds of trouble. My cousin Jackie and I would put her little brother, Billy, in my snow sled, and push him off the top bunk. It was pandemonium. And we loved every minute of it.

We made the biggest fuss in three separate States when our parents told us that wasn't happening anymore. We felt betrayed. I remember declaring, *how could you do this to us!?* We laugh about it, now.

But back to just three outfits. I was demoralized. Three outfits? Three!? How was I going to make that work? My mom suggested that I simply add the best clothes out of what I already had to my new ones and mix and match. I was exasperated. Madness! It was sheer madness, I thought. Primal, unadulterated madness.

When the first week of school arrived, I did my best to camouflage that, unlike other kids, I only had three new outfits. I wore a new outfit the first three days, and then, mixed in an old shirt with new pants on the fourth, and an old pair of pants with a new shirt from the first day, on the fifth.

No one noticed. Not a single person.

I was both relieved and troubled. I remember thinking, on the fifth day, *what's wrong with you people?* CAN'T YOU SEE I'M WEARING OLD CLOTHES?

Today, I look back at it with amusement. I still love clothes. I still like to look good—stylish, not fashionable. There's a difference. I've been to thrift stores and discount warehouses —I thank my broke college years for introducing me to that. I didn't have a father around. So I learned how to tie my own tie, how much break should be in pant's cuffs, the philosophy behind suspenders or belt, shining my shoes, and you leave the botton button of your suit coat and vest unbuttoned. And so much more. The difference between style and fashion. How much of your shirt cuff should peek out of your coat sleeve. And that buying one pair of expensive shoes, that could be resoled, was better than constantly buying cheap ones. All this was complicated by the inevitable difficulties of navigating a country, as a black man, where people presumed you were indigent, looking to steal, untrustworthy, or unable to afford the merchandize in a store. But that's another story. Most importantly, I grew to understand that clothes don't actually make the man. All of it was a journey into self-discovery, tied up in self-worth, and personal expression.

Eventually, it dawned on young me that I saw the world very differently from many of my peers. I realized the things that mattered to me didn't necessarily matter to everyone else. Only later did I also understand they were *white* and subject to other exigencies and expectations. I learned I had a mother who was gracious enough to put up with my developing sensibilities, while still being responsible enough to tell me the truth. We never had a lot, by other people's standards. She never bought me $300 sneakers, or a whole new wardrobe every school year. But she kept us fed, clothed, safe, and showered in love. And, ultimately, that was all that mattered.

gas light

the hubris
is breathtaking
it's ozymandius
with an opioid
addiction
high on
whiteness
though
i understand
why you do it
shame
is inescapable
even when you
don't
believe in it

watching you
do it
is wild though
because you either
think
we don't understand it
or you're going
to get away with it
anyway
a mugging
in broad daylight
a lie so

laughable
you must actually
believe
we're stupid

desperate
to rewrite
history
so you aren't
the villain
as if words
in a textbook
can wash
blood
off your hands

you want to erase
the trail
of devastation
you've left
in your wake
across history
as if
it's not written
in our
dna

maybe
if you weren't
still cashing checks
on *wounded knee*
transferring funds

from *tulsa*
you could
get away with it
but
the blood money
is still
in your pocket

depraved but indifferent

the show
must go on
how else do we
explain
having the nerve
to show up
at the U. N.

in our blackface
painted on in
the limo
shuffling across the
floor of the
general assembly, while
we do our jig
doffing our straw
hat at perestroika
detente and the arab
spring, with
a spit shine
on our spats
mugging for the
cameras while "bullshit"
is muttered by
193 delegates in
six official languages
in response to

our tap dance
on an overturned
koch industries soap
box, to the tune
strange fruit
we burp out a
strongly worded protest
against human rights
violations
that smell like
a big mac and fries

that smell like normalcy, gluttony, a treat

all the while
the accused delegates
of the evil member
countries, roll their
eyes and go back to
reading the new york
times, where it
says eric garner
was choked to death
by the police for
selling loose
cigarettes

"the new Jim Code"
  - how are injustices being
  replicated across time?

on praxes shore we lie

in the wasteland
of conscience
apathy reigns
a king
without an army
or throne
but a crown
of plastic
perched askew
a head
empty of history
hollow
as the word
of sympathy
uttered
from the comfort
of the same whiteness
that plagues
the countryside

how long?

red summer

By the God of Heaven, we are cowards and jackasses
if now that the war is over, we do not marshal every
ounce of our brain and brawn to fight a sterner, longer,
more unbending battle against the forces of hell in our
own land.
~ *W. E. B. Du Bois*

it was 1919
and
james weldon johnson
called it
the red
summer
but
it was mostly
our blood

from chicago
to d. c.
to elaine, arkansas
and everywhere
in between
your grandparents
and their parents
murdered black folks
in the street
burning

our worlds
to the ground
because that's
who you were
(and are?)

every time
we built
swing sets and
family rooms
lunch counters
and work desks
you showed up
frothing
at the mouth
with no other
writ or cause
but hate

the blood
of our children
will not wash
off your hands
with soap
or by forbidding
teachers
from talking
about us
because we
will never
forget
especially when

both surface level solutions (handwritten annotation)

you try so hard
to

even now
you dance
on their graves
by wondering aloud
why we have
no wealth
to speak of
as if you didn't
burn it all down
with a grin
as if
passing years
and bleach
erase
blood stains
on souls

in the summer
of 1919
you burned
our worlds
to the ground
just like you had
before
and since
and i wonder
is that
why you're so
afraid?

because you know
the bill
is due

(The Red Summer violence and massacres:
Washington and Norfolk July 19-23, Jenkins
County, Georgia April 13 – July 14, Charleston
May 10, Longview, Texas early July, Bisbee,
Arizona July 3, Garfield Park, Indianapolis July
14, Chicago July 27 – August 12, Knoxville,
Tennessee August 30-31, Omaha, Nebraska
September 28-29, Elaine, Arkansas September
30, Wilmington, Delaware November 13)

on the electrodynamics of

moving bodies

einstein said
that time
is relative
that *two events,*
simultaneous for one observer,
may not be simultaneous
for another observer
if the observers are in
relative motion

you seem to think
as louie sang
that you have
all
the time
in the world

my mama's
been waiting
to be included
to get a decent
interest rate
on a mortgage
to not be
redlined
out of a neighborhood

my grandfather
waited
to be seen
as a man
not
a boy
to have room
to be angry
to feel
the full spectrum
of human emotions
without it
being
a death sentence
and he died waiting

my great grandfather
waited
to be allowed
to vote
to put his hand
on the wheel
that turns
the world
without
the threat
of hoods
and burning crosses
without
the manifest
horror

of people
who thought
they were better
than him
that he had
no soul

i'm waiting
to be able
to breathe
to shop
to have lunch
to sit on my porch
without the specter
of white
presumption
of whether
i have a right
to be
anywhere
without
showing my papers
or dying
because you
are scared

we have
waited
four hundred
years
to have our humanity
matter

while you
keep saying
just a little while
longer
that you need
to catch up
before
justice can be
served

james baldwin
said it
best

how much time do you need?

INTERLUDE three

cardboard and dreams

I loved cardboard boxes. If there was anything that ignited the fires of my imagination as a kid, it was a giant cardboard box. They were responsible for my Captain America shield, made of several layers duck taped together, painted appropriately, and throwable. A Bat Cave style computer console, and a spaceship in which I traveled to distant galaxies.

A cardboard box was nearly responsible for my premature death. I was inside it, playing in my driveway, when my uncle came to visit. He nearly ran over it with me inside. He only managed to see it, and stop, because it started moving.

Whenever I saw a cardboard box, I immediately began to dream about possibilities. What could I make? What thing had I seen in a cartoon or comic that I could now replicate. What supplies would I need? Spray paint? Duct tape, obviously. Rope? Wheels? Markers? One summer I made two fighter jets.

The first one, I made during my only visit to see my father in Detroit. In my entire life, I'd seen him only a half a dozen times. The entire inventory of my inheritance from him amounted to $25 and a chess set. He was responsible for nearly all the anger and emotional turmoil I suffer as a child. I wanted a father, and he was never around. It got bad enough in the 5th grade that my teacher, Ms. Blakeman, noticed and sent a note home to my mom. I had grown despondent. My grades began to drop, and she stepped in like a good teacher. I loved Ms. Blakeman. I'd lay, unconscious, under her chair during nap time. I asked her, on a field trip, to wait for me to get older, so I could marry her. She laughed and told me how flattered she was and that she'd be very old when I got old enough to get married. She was a great teacher.

My brother and I had gotten big enough to be a real handful for my mom. We were fighting and being as generally disruptive as two teen boys could be. So, she decided it was time for my absent father to pitch in and she put us on a bus to Detroit to spend the summer with him. It was a disaster.

He was never around, even with us in his house. He was basically a landlord who came home long enough to shower and leave again. He'd leave us a few dollars for lunch, and we wouldn't see him again until the next day. And when he was around? He was leaving us in the car to score drugs, or he was running around town meeting up with the many women he was seeing, expecting us to be mum on the subject.

The singular highlight was his purchase of a home entertainment system that came with a massive set of cardboard boxes. When I asked him what he was going to do with them he shrugged and said he was throwing them away. When I asked if I could have them, he shrugged again and said, yeah.

metaphor for turning/repurposing trauma into something beautiful →

I spent the next several hours making a fighter jet. It had wings, a canopy I could pull down over the pilot's seat, and wheels. I made a flight stick and controls. And once it was finished, I got in it and imagined I was in the middle of dog fights ala the tv show, *Baa Baa Black Sheep*.

His "main" girlfriend was impressed. She gushed over it. She commended me for my creatively and said she loved it. He didn't care. She tried to get him to engage whenever she was over to the house, to get him to act like a father with his sons, but he was unavailable emotionally or in any other way.

We called home several times to get Mom to let us come home. It was only when my brother told her my father was buying drugs that she decided the experiment was over. We boarded another bus and made the terminally long trip, hitting every back road availabe to greyhound.

Certainly, there was emotional fallout. I was angry with him for being what he was. And angry with my mom for subjecting us to it. But that was the last time I gave him a chance to act like a real father. It was also when I realized he was no longer worth it.

Later that summer my mom purchased a washer or dryer, or some appliance that came in a massive cardboard box. I don't remember exactly what because I only had eyes for the cardboard. So, I decided to make another fighter jet.

It was even more complex than the earlier version. It still had a canopy and wings, but they were detachable so I could store the whole thing in the pantry. I would wheel it out into the living room, or the driveway, so I could soar above the clouds, engaging my enemies in aerial combat. I'd imagine being swarmed by enemies—a bird surrounded by bees ticking off their numbers as I took them down one at a time, watching them splash down in the ocean below.

I'm sure it was a mixture of escapism, therapeutic coping mechanisms, and my unbridled creativity. But my imagination, buoyed by novels, comic books, and animation, was a fire that warmed me. I visited distant worlds, fought unimaginable creatures with a sword, rode on the back of dragons, played at being a gunslinger in the old west, pretended to be a hero with superpowers, and captained a star ship. And all of it was aided by a little bit of cardboard.

great depression

a soup kitchen
is not
responsible
for a full
heart
even if
you only have
empty feelings
at home

besides
they're closed
at night

assuming you are owed a
solution for x, a.k.a algebra
when basic arithmetic won't
do

maybe
your understanding of algebra
is the problem

you
are not owed
access
behind the curtain
that divides
my public performance
from
the naked
i, reserved
for the people
i show
my heartbeat
the places it hurts
what my laughter
sounds like
when no one can hear me

in quadratic equations
the x is
unknown
and mine is not
owed to you

just because
we have coffee
and a secret
does not mean
i have signed up
to fill your empty spaces
or be more
than a tangent
on your
curve

you can call it
unseemly
that a man
decides to hold
that reservation
for a certain
woman
or somehow
a revocation
of a social contract
he never signed
but when did
you start confusing
variables and constants?

it was always
a polynomial expression

just because we laughed
at the same
joke
and share
an inestimable desire
to run silently
in the darkness
with bits of
other people's souls
on the bottom
of our shoes
does not mean
i am willing
to circle
your squared parts

you are not
owed

if
you cannot
get that at home
maybe
you should move

shrug

i don't
care enough
about
what you think
to
write a whole poem
about
how i'm
not like
those other men
i
can't even
bring myself
to finish
this

missing andry

i wonder
what you taste
like

coffee and powdered beignet
at 2 am
on a new orleans
side street
or red wine and
hoppin john
under the moonlight
in gratz park
with your lips
on mine

will i be
hungry for you
dizzy on miles
or cool
with coltrane spinning
my head around
the sanguine luster
of your heated breath
in my ear
the warmth
of your lips
on my neck

round about midnight
will i be as lost
in you
as monk was on stage
in paris
a whole ass mood
as i reach
your sweet
spot
with my tongue

will we get
lost
in freshly tangled
sheets
abandoned
playing in the
background
the hard and soft
of sweat
come by honestly
until i explode
in you
like
a galaxy
being born

will you
hold my hand
on the rocky
streets
outside snake

and jakes
not just because
you're wearing heels
but my soul
while you tell me
forbidden words
in a forbidden tongue
while the rest
of the world
fades away
as we stare
at each other
until the universe
burns out

it's a cool
autumn night
and my heart
beats a little
faster
to the song
of crickets
in the wood
as i wonder

what you taste like

the little things *→major tonal shift*

some believe
diamonds are
rare
but
they would be
wrong
their market
is artificially
inflated by
hoarding
they are the
product
of clever
marketing
just like some
people
i know

in 1951
painite
was discovered
and
for decades
only two existed

in the whole
of the world
glistening in
faceted glory
and that
is what
i think of
when i
think of you

not because
you are
beautiful
the form
your shape
takes
in the light
of the morning
how a sheer
gown
falls
across your
slender shoulders
to rounded
hips
like verdant hills
on the horizon
or the light
brown eyes
one might fall
into
when looking

at them
the long brown
hair
one might want
to feel
brush
across your
chest and face
at twilight

there are
a million
beautiful women
in the world

it's because
of how you
walk through
the world
how you
tilt your head
just so
how you
know
what you want
how you talk
about
what's important
to you
and all
the little intoxicating
things

that make you
who
you are

you are
a thousand
miles away
like a moon
in orbit
but i see you
and how
rare
you are

want

there is a
moment
when i know
you
want me

they say
time
is a construct
unreal
a fabrication
of our minds
as we try
to
make sense
of the cosmos
but in that
moment
when your eyes
change
the way
they look at
me
and i imagine
your body
warm
against mine
that time

seems as real
as
my blood
rushing away
from my heart
to other
places
in my body

i know
you want me
like a predator
eyeing its
prey
and i drop
a place
on the food
chain
as you lick
your lips
considering
where you will
start
devouring me
with no regard
for time of
day
or place
your hands
tell me
the floor
is just as good

a place
as any
and you will not
stop
until you are
satisfied
sweaty
exhausted
because i won't
let go
until i hear you
exhale

i know you want
me
despite taboo
public opinion
or what anyone
has to
say
and the truth is
i
want you
too

the morning after

cum
let me lick you
around the edges
and down the
middle
like a stamp

i will mail you
back to reality
in the morning
naked
covered in dew
smiling
smelling like
me

INTERLUDE four

friday night dice

Friday nights were for D&D. Sometime early in the 70s, (1974) Gary Gygax and Dave Arneson published the first books for their new RPG (role playing game). I don't remember what prompted me to stop in at the Rusty Scabbard when it was located right next to Woodland Park, but it was likely because someone told me about it. They had comics, miniatures, all kinds of geek paraphernalia, and the materials for a new, little known game called Dungeons & Dragons.

D&D seeped into the life of nerds like me —surreptitiously. It was, after the fact, a given for Saturday morning cartoon—comic book devourers. We weren't watching heroes or reading about them, we were them. What could be more enticing?

I remember purchasing my first Players Handbook. I read through it in astonishment.

Here was a game that was going to allow me to become a fighter, thief, wizard, bard, or cleric. I would creep through dungeons, fight dragons, cast spells, or carry a sword. There were hit points, armor classes, and lots of dice. It was fascinating. Once I found some fellow adherents, it became hours and hours of unbridled fun. We leveraged our imaginations to envision ourselves doing things we read about in sword and sorcery novels or Conan comics.

Friday nights became our night. We'd assemble in our kitchen with friends. We'd lay out our array of books, character sheets, and dice. My mom would order pizza, supply us with 2-liter drinks, and leave us to our own devices. Remarkably, she never bothered us. Even when our gaming marathons went to midnight or one in the morning. I discovered later that she loved it. She had teen boys and was glad to know exactly where we were on a Friday night. So, the expense of feeding all of us and the concomitant noise we would conjur until late at night didn't matter to her one bit. In her mind, it was an easy trade. She knew we were safe at home and not running the streets like other teenagers our age.

I made some great friends playing D&D. And it was a fertile ground for our burgeoning imaginations. In a lot of ways, it was like a little club of like-minded co-conspirators. We'd talk endlessly, for days, about the shenanigans we got up to in-game, recounting the funny, heroic, and the absurd—laughing about falling into traps, being blown up by our resident wizard, and rolling Nat 1's or 20's at crucial moments.

I look back now and realize on many occasions we didn't even play. We spent hours rolling new characters, but ended up just talking. We ate pizza, tacos, hot dogs, whole bags of chips, and hamburgers. Someone would mention the new issue of the X-men or the newest cartoons—the movie Beastmaster, Time Bandits, or Conan starring Arnold, and we'd be off discussing it only to eventually realize it was too late to start a campaign in earnest. So, we'd pack up and promise to actually play next time.

Those were formative, and as some might say—halcyon—days mixed with arcades, BMX bikes, and Chuck Taylor sneakers. It was a time of relative innocence in a lot of ways. Before the inherent biases and toxicity of fandom washed in to invade the preciousness of our space. We were just kids having fun, playing at epic fantasy, who really just enjoyed a camaraderie based on shared love of all things science fiction and fantasy. We were of the same tribe, and we recognized ourselves in one another.

Today, I'm a science fiction and fantasy writer as much as I am a poet. I'm certain Dungeons & Dragons contributed to that. And when I find myself at Science Fiction & Fantasy conventions plying my trade as an author, I once again see my tribe. I can tell the fighters from the wizards, the barbarians from the paladins, the thieves from the rogues and clerics. And we still sit up late at night talking about our love of all things epic fantasy. The only difference now is that it's bourbon instead of orange soda in our glasses.

quantum entanglement

is there a universe
where you are my twin
in swirling fire and blazing
light
in bravery
not unafraid
but
willing to court
disaster
in the hope
that delicious monogamy
awaits
those who dare
to dance naked
before one another

meet me
between the up
and down quarks
i'll be wearing
a red
carnation

the substance of things
hoped for

i live
on possibly
that you just
haven't
found me yet

it can be
lonely
but
i believe
in you
and the possibility
that you're on
your way
to our collision
with love
and you are merely
delayed
not
impossible

while i
wait
dreaming
of you

i stretch
into wisdom
expanding
into joy
evolving
into the best
version
of me
knowing it will make you
smile
that your partner
in all things

will be ready when you arrive

brown - eyed girls

(for every one of you)

brown-eyed
girls
make the world
go round
like the corner
piece
of a pan of brownies
a sleeve
of girl scout
cookies
or the law
of conservation
of energy
comforting me
that joy cannot
be destroyed
it simply changes
form

brown-haired girls
make
the sun shine
like
hopping in puddles
ice cream on
noses
or getting shit done
mending

the world
and making it
safe
for brown skin
boys

we don't
bring out
the confetti
the bright lights
the stars
in our eyes
for
brown-eyed girls
even when
they are kindly
completely
saving
the world

painted lady

a few precious
weeks
is all
they are granted
to flitter in
the sunlight
with wings fit
for a queen
and then
like a warm summer
evening breeze
that brushes by you
kissing your face
like a possible
lover
before disappearing
around the corner
they are gone
and you are left
with only
what might have been
crumpled in your
palm
like a receipt
from the universe
that says
nonrefundable

she should have had more time

stardust

(for marianne)

you are
stardust
acquainted
with the enduring dance
of the galaxy
its waxing and waning
affair
with gravitational
love
its flux and flair
the solemnity
of the interstellar
twinkles
in your eyes
like a thousand stars
circling
a million planets
and one
brown man

you are
sunlight
spun like
silken radiance
on a terrestrial
loom of kindness

the gentle humanity
of your
warp and weft
alighting
on the right angles
of your soft
smile
a stray comet
passing through
the darkened
constellation
of a solitary
star gazer

thank you
for how brightly
you light up
the night

port in a storm

(for Ola)

they say
any port
in a storm
but that
isn't true

when you are
black
joy
can become
horror
in the sliver
of space
between a smile
and a sneer
especially
when one
isn't
meant for you
but the other
is
especially
when
you thought
you could leave
your life jacket
at home

because you thought
the water
was safe

a typhoon
of *i am*
better than
you
and *you are not*
human
can appear
over the horizon
before
the clouds even
darken
to warn you
that you
are its target

latitude and longitude
circumscribed
by ego
surrounding you
with surging waves
of transgression
hollowing winds
of presumption
meant to overwhelm
you
in hopelessness
or infamy
to drown you

watch you flail
in powerlessness
gulping for air
that has been
sucked
from the room
by someone
oblivious
to your
pain

and you can
suffer
in silence
black man
because to rage
righteous as that
may be
is to
become
the
villain
especially
if they are
old
white
female

but you
saw me
drowning
frozen

in a why
i could not
understand
a what
i could not
believe
a choice
i could not
make
swallowed
in waves of grief
winds of fury
wounded
alone
bereft
betrayed
like othello
in a cyprus
i did not
ask or expect
to visit
not among
friends

and you
wrapped me up
in love

a hurricane
of
incandescent
unwavering

warmth
safe arms
and soft lips
that blew me
into the eye
of the storm
threatening
to crush
my spirit
carrying me
to dry land
and
standing
between me
and a world
hostile
to my blackness
my right
to be whole
unmolested

you stood
there
until
i could breathe
shining
on me
like the light
of a thousand
thousand stars
until my hands
were no longer

fists
my eyes
were dry
until
i stopped shaking

and for that
i will never
stop
loving you

do not
believe them
when they say
any port
in a storm
because
when you are black
you can
drown
on dry
land
and the port
matters more
than the storm

the quintessential thing

we pretend as though
other things matter
the music score
the dribble of time
at that unavoidable shore
the coin of the realm
that favored film
a taste upon the tongue
that glass we filled
but we are cigar smoke
floating on the wind
a heavy billowing mass
evaporating as we speak
never to be seen again
lost to the long enduring
darkness
recalled only by those
who loved us so
      and what remains?

we act as though
so much matters
so much
of things
of words
and impressions
firsts and lasts

thought indelible
irrevocable
eternal under the heavens
but we are ripples
on a pond
lost in a wood
here
and then gone
eternally
into an unfathomable deep
remembered only
by those we laughed or cried with
who we hold onto
like a piece of sunken ship
in the middle of an unending sea
           and what remains?

so
here is
the truth of it all
for what time is left
before the universe falls
unraveled into a quantum
fray
up quarks and down
whose excitation has faded
rolled up like a shrinking violet
at the far end
of time
ending in silence
an existential dread
with no witness

to mourn its passing
save her everlasting self
a divine shrug
or a holy sigh
possibly prodded
to start it all again
with another fortuitous bang
chastened
by the knowledge of what
has gone before
while we all rest
in ignoble ignorance
beyond all tears
breaths
or heartbeats
the only thing
left to echo
through the vastness
of the unending void
a single, quintessential
thing
which makes any of it
worthwhile

that we loved

a multiverse of madness

(on the occasion of the buffalo massacre)

we are
a
multiverse
by necessity
it is how
we survive
without
going mad
or curling up
in a corner
and turning
our power
off

when you know
you can be
murdered
for being
black
in a grocery store
accosted
for sweeping
your front porch
or bird watching
suffocated to death
on the street

[handwritten annotation: Such an interesting way to talk about double consciousness → learning to survive in multiple universes]

in front of
a crowd
of onlookers
by people
who claim
to embody
safety
you learn to
divide your soul
into multiple
universes
or you'd unravel
like an object
entering
the event horizon
of a black
hole

do not confuse
our calm
or smile
with peace
or
unfettered joy
because
the world
we live in
orbits must
not may
our
choices
are not legion

or
voluntary

some days
i wonder
what living
the lives
we are forced into
would do
to you
could you survive?
or would you
be left listless
a white
dwarf star
unable to maintain
its integrity
resigned to being
a celestial shadow
of your
former self
incapable
of radiating light
or heat

you see us
perform
this miracle
everyday
dressing ourselves
in
sheer will

walking
into
a hostile environment
not meant
to sustain
life
splitting atoms
just to make it
through the day
and you think
this shit
is easy

it's quantum
fucking
mechanics
and also
madness

consistent thread in collection

postlude

kumite

When I was concluding my work on the hardcover edition of **NAPPY** *metaphysic*, another whirlwind of extra-legal murders of black folks took place. Breonna Taylor was murdered in her home by cops who bungled a no-knock warrant. George Floyd was murdered by a cop who knelt on his neck for an excruciatingly horrific amount of time until Floyd was dead. Ahmaud Arbery was hunted down and murdered by three white men while he was out jogging.

It was all too much.

I did what I normally do in the face of this kind of trauma, aside from feeling rage – I wrote about it. I decided to add the suite of poems that came from that experience to the hardcover edition of **NAPPY**.

As I was preparing this collection, a very different kind of event took place. Two famous, and wealthy, black men were involved in a public assault, on one of the biggest stages in all of entertainment. I decided to conclude **ON THE BLACK HAND SIDE** with some reflections on the matter.

My brother is over six feet tall. I realized early on that wasn't going to be. Once that was clear, I knew that if I wasn't ever going to be the biggest guy in a fight, I'd be the most skilled. I embarked on a decades long journey into the martial arts.

It became a trip through a host of cultures, techniques, and disciplines. I went from wrestling, to boxing, to Shotokan, Tae Kwon Do, Wing Chun, Aikido, Fencing, and dabbling some martial forms that I won't mention here. Suffice it to say, I became well acquainted with the application of violence. But there are two things I'm especially grateful for having learned, and a third I'll share.

First, I can take a punch (or kick as the case may be). It's something that changes you. It acquaints you, intimately, with who you really are. I've seen two basic responses to people getting hit for the very first time. You either step forward or you step back. In other words, it tells you a lot about who you are.

I learned early on that there was a deep reservoir of rage inside me. It's not a wild, indiscriminate rage. It only showed up when someone tried to hurt me. Whether I was in the ring, on the mat, in the Sol, the Dojo, the Dojang, or in the streets, if you hit me, I was always going to step forward.

The second thing I learned was how to control that impulse. I'm deeply grateful for it.

I learned how to decide when I was going to deploy violence and, more importantly, how not to. You see, what great teachers in the martial arts teach you is self-control and discipline. It taught me I didn't have anything to prove.

I've been in many situations, over the years, where a guy was standing across from me shouting and cussing or talking about what he was going to do to me. A lesser man takes that bait and initiates violence. But I learned how to spot the fear in the performance. It made me feel sorry for them more than anything. And because I knew what I was capable of, how skilled I was, how prepared I was to physically take them apart, it removed the fear from the moment, and allowed me to feel unthreatened in the moment.

You can tell when someone if actually going to hit you and when they are just barking loud for the people watching, even if the only person watching is you. I learned how to stay calm and wait.

You see, the third thing I learned is where my line is. And where most people's line should be. You can bark all day. It doesn't bother me. It's only when you try to put your hands on me that you've crossed a line. And that's when things get serious. There is one exception to my rule I should mention.

Hate speech.

I have no problem with punching a nazi, or someone using the N-word. I believe these people are engaged in a very specific, and particular, type of act, which goes well beyond the ordinary limits of speech. They are engaged in a call to violent action against marginalized people and they should be met with swift and appropriate action.

I remember my mother making it clear, when I was young, that a mom joke was not an excuse for me to get in a fight. She didn't care about a joke, and she made sure I understood that I wasn't to care either. She had no patience for being called to school over some foolishness.

I don't believe a joke, or most other forms of speech, are a justification for violence. I wouldn't be in a relationship with a woman who wanted me to risk jail, or worse, because someone said something about them. But every woman I've ever been close to knew that if someone tried to put their hands on them, I'd be there to step in with the appropriate amount of force.

I'm deeply disappointed in the number of people I saw defending the act of violence so many of us either watched live or, like me, on video after the fact. A very smart friend of mine, a black woman, made an incredibly astute assessment of it all. She pointed out how many people were responding out of their own personal pathology, and I agree. People who felt like they'd never been protected by a significant other, or the culture at large, agreed with it. Men who wanted to look tough agreed with it.

But like her, all I saw was a sad display of pathology playing out in front of millions of people. And despite the immediate applause by some, the person who committed the assault is now having to live with the consequences, despite his apology tour after the fact. It also interesting that the people who applauded him have somehow managed to overlook his apologies and condemnation of his own behavior.

I'm thankful that I learned about violence in the way I did. It has managed to keep me in a healthy place, psychologically, and helped me know when the application of violence was necessary. But more importantly, it taught me when walking away was the more honorable, reasonable, and responsible thing to do.

"He will win who knows when to fight and when not to fight."
~ Sun Tzu, The Art of War

acknowledgements

ON THE BLACK HAND SIDE would not be possible without the help and support of a lot of people. I want to thank my family for their support, especially my mother and brother. Choosing to be a writer is tough in the society we live in. It would be even tougher if my family was pushing for me to do something else.

I want to thank my fellow Affrilachian poets for their friendship and support. Finding a community of writers all those years ago was instrumental in giving me the courage to claim the name *poet*.

A very special thanks to every who contributed to the kickstarter that made publishing this collection possible:

Milton Davis, Allison Charlesworth, Sean Hillman, Blaze Ward, Sarah, Rina Wesel, Bracken MacLeaod, Ross Newberry, Heather Lewis, Scott Wilson, Dana Cameron, Ola Jacunski, Liz Giordano, Ahmad Williams, Joe Hilliard, Judy Dillon, Daryle Cobb, Jon Hermsen, Thomas DeSimone, Kathy Gosnell, Kelly Keuneke-Marts, Selene, John Woodcock, Jennifer Halbman, Kristine Yohe, Robert Greene, Roni Jonah, Rachel Brune, Richard Fife, Reese Hogan, Claudia Wair, Jacqueline Mitchell, Sara Hinson

Bond, Erin Underwood, Robert Saffell, Jeffery T. Johnson, Maggie May Schill, William Akin, Ashley Chappell, Melanie R. Meadors, Rachel Little, Dragonsteel Books, and every who donated but who may not have wanted their names listed. Thank you. This wouldn't be possible without you.

about the author

Gerald L. Coleman is a philosopher, theologian, poet, and Science Fiction & Fantasy Author. He was born in Lexington and now makes his home in the Atlanta area. He did his undergraduate work in philosophy, english, and religious studies, followed by a Master's degree in Theology. He is the author of the Epic Fantasy novel saga *The Three Gifts*, which currently includes *When Night Falls* (Book One), *A Plague of Shadows* (Book Two), and the upcoming *When Chaos Reigns* (Book Three). His most recent poetry appears in *Pluck! The Journal of Affrilachian Arts & Culture, Drawn To Marvel: Poems From The Comic Books, Pine Mountain Sand & Gravel Vol. 18, Black Bone Anthology, the 10th Anniversary Issue of Diode Poetry Journal, About Place Journal,* and *Star*line Vol. 43, Issue 4.* His speculative fiction short stories appear in: The Cyberfunk Anthology: *The City,* the *Rococoa* Anthology by Roaring Lion, the Urban Fantasy Anthology: *Terminus,* the 2019 JordanCon Anthology: *You Want Stories?, Dark Universe: Bright Empire, Cyberfunk!* by MVMedia, and *Whether Change: The Revolution Will Be Weird.* His most recent essay appears in the science fiction & fantasy publication Apex Magazine. He has been a Guest Author at DragonCon, Boskone, Blacktasticon, JordanCon, Atlanta Science Fiction & Fantasy Expo, The Outer Dark Symposium, World Horror Con, Imaginarium, and Multiverse. He is a Scholastic National Writing Juror, a co-founder of the Affrilachian Poets, an SFWA member, and a Rhysling Award Nominee. He is currently working on new editions of When Night Falls, A Plague of Shadows, and writing book three in the epic fantasy series - entitled, When Chaos Reigns. You can find him at Geraldcoleman.com.

Printed in the USA
CPSIA information can be obtained
at www.ICGtesting.com
LVHW040435100823
754785LV00004B/622

9 781087 868592